This Book Belongs TO

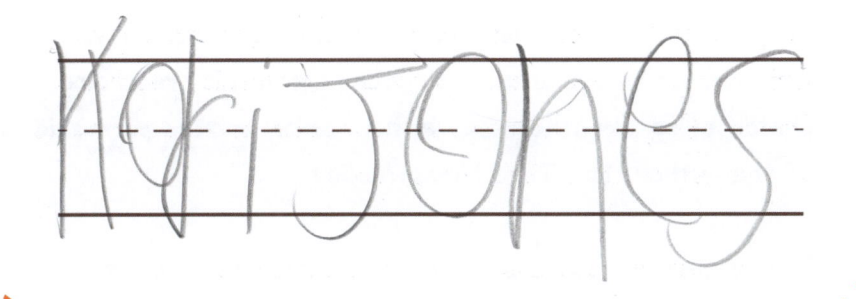

Kori Jones

Kori,
Dream BIG!
Dr. Dara

ISBN: 978-0-578-38332-3
Scripting With Scriptures
©2022
Dr. Tara Hines-McCoy. All Rights Reserved.
Published by Dr. Tara Hines-McCoy.

No part of this book may be reproduced or transmitted in any form or by any means, written, electronic, recording, photocopying, or otherwise, without prior written permission of the author, Dr. Tara Hines-McCoy.

For permission requests, solicit the author via the email address below
Tjaienterprises, LLC
DBA: DRTARASPEAKS
drtara@drtaraspeaks.com

Printed in the United States of America

Dedication

I would not know anything about the love of God if it were not for my loving parents Arthur & Paula Hines. They gave me the first introduction to the goodness and faithfulness of God through their unwavering example of being parents but most of all as a man and woman after God's own heart. I am eternally grateful to God for choosing you as parents for ME.

To my late grandmother, Emma Mae Bondon Cohns, who was an avid writer of letters to family and friends. I am eternally grateful for your words of encouragment, wisdom, and most of all prayers.

To my Jai'Renee. As I have the pleasure of raising you, you have also raised me. I've learned more from you as a single parent than any class could offer. I will never take for granted the honor of being your mother. It is truly the biggest career flex I will ever have.

Aa

ADAM

"Adam is the first man God created"

ADAM

adam

ANGEL

a

apple

Scripture of the day

Practice the scripture by tracing over each of the letters below.

In the beginning God created the heavens and the earth.
Genesis 1:1

Bb

BIBLE

"The Bible is God's stories and messages for us"

BIBLE

bible

B

BOOK

bread

Scripture of the day

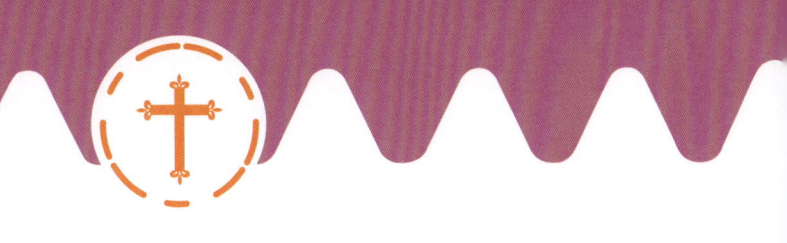

Practice the scripture by tracing over each of the letters below.

Jesus wept.

Jesus wept.

Jesus wept.

John 11:35

Cc

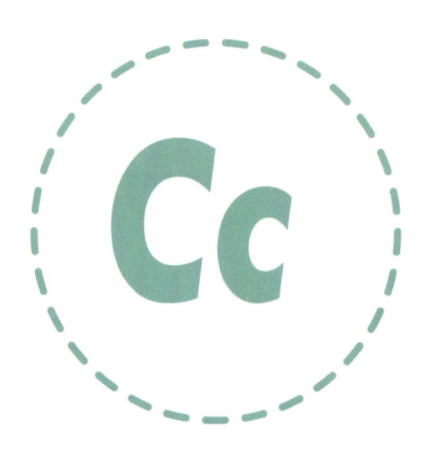

CHRIST

"Christ is the savior and Messiah"

CHRIST

christ

C

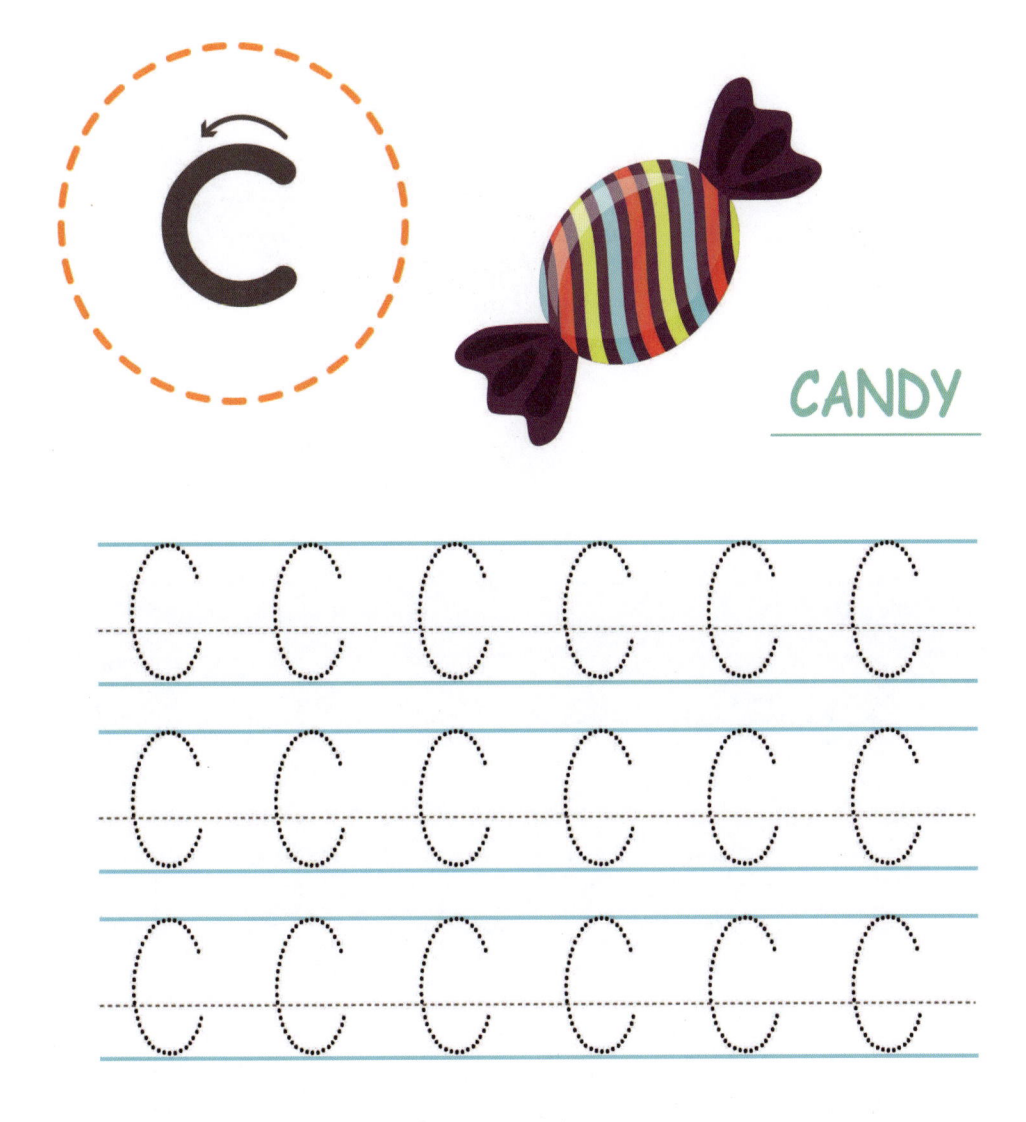

CANDY

c

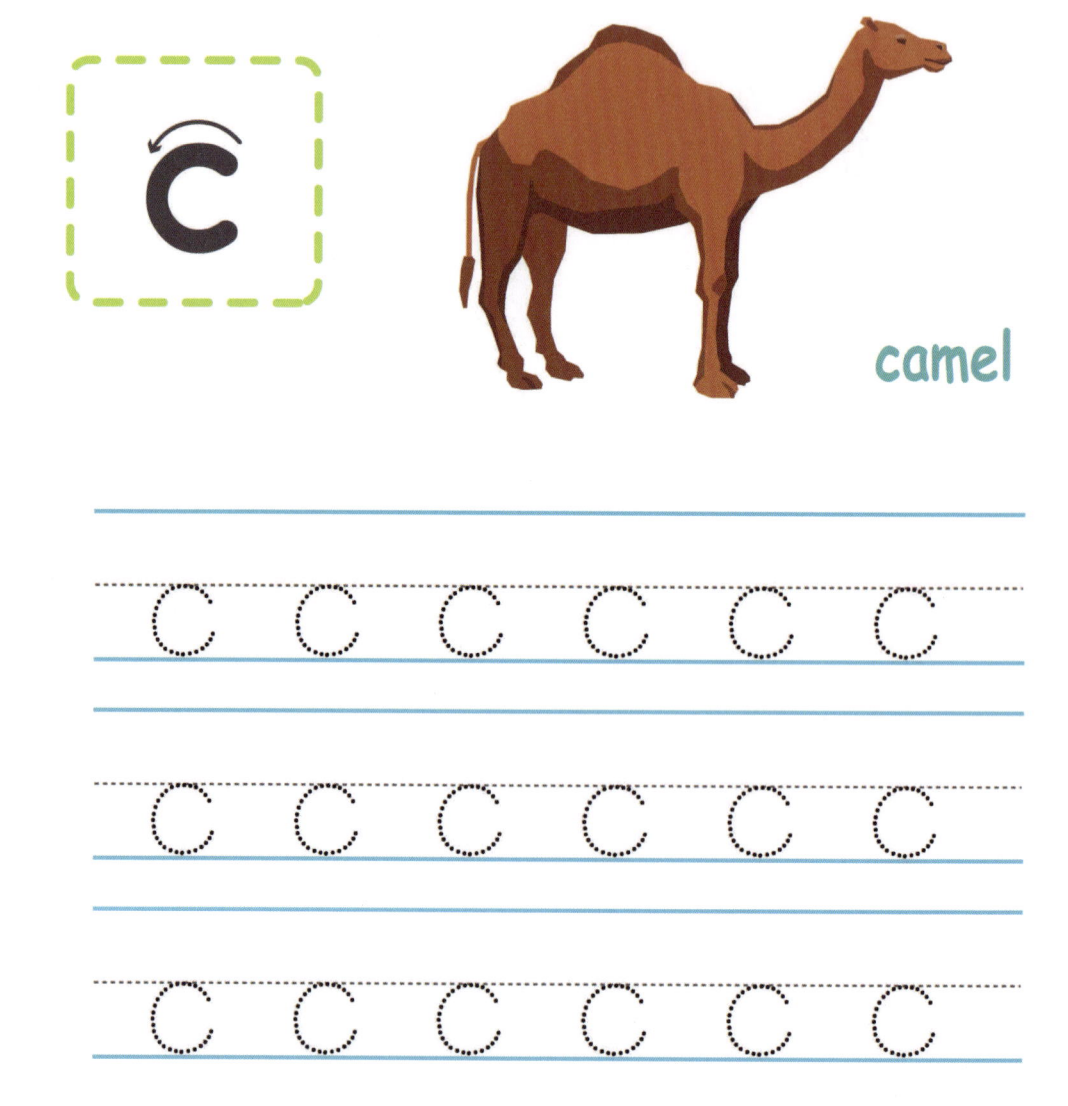

camel

c c c c c c

c c c c c c

c c c c c c

Scripture of the day

Practice the scripture by tracing over each of the letters below.

I am the bread of life

John 6:48

Dd

DAVID

"David is a man after God's heart"

DAVID

david

D

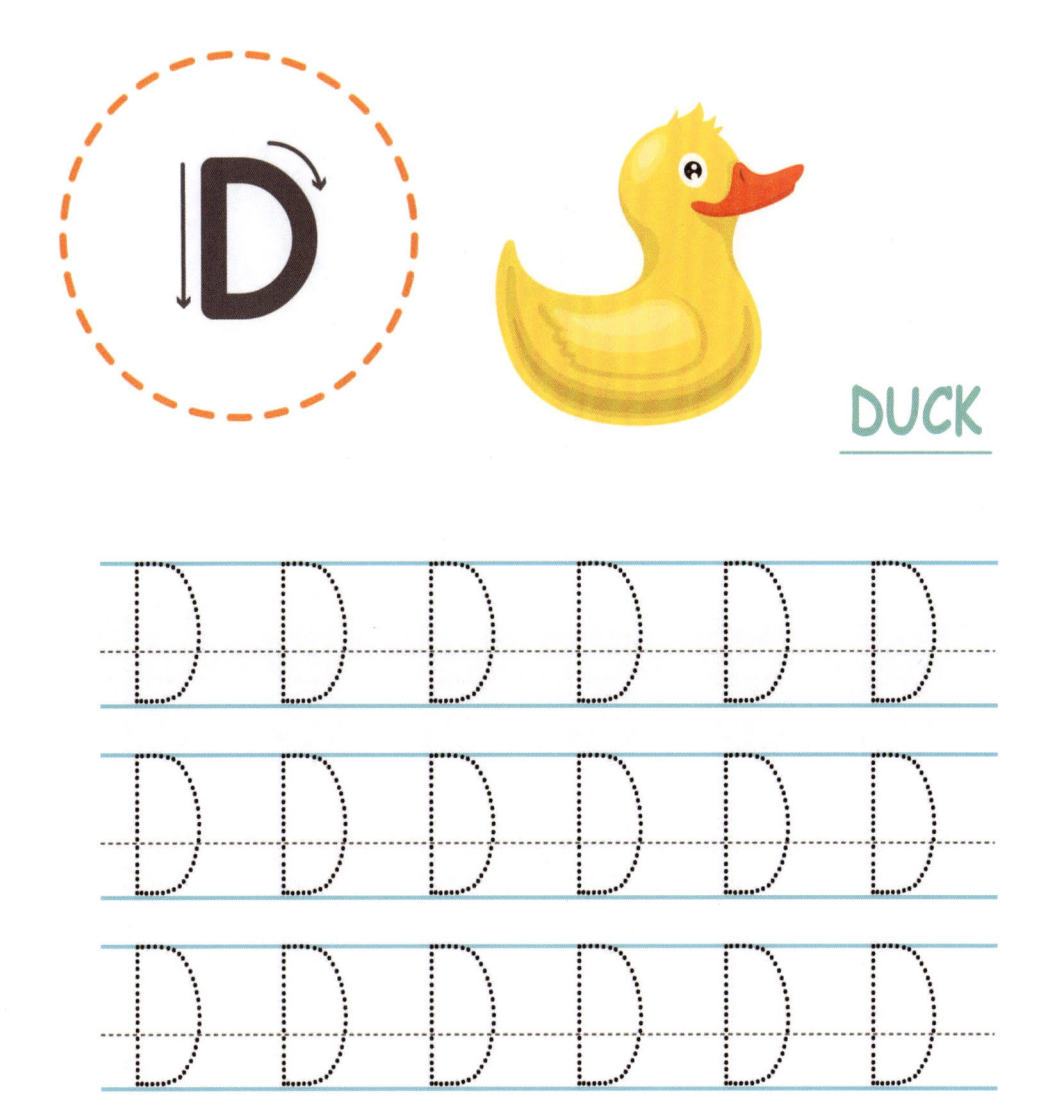

DUCK

donkey

Scripture of the day

Practice the scripture by tracing over each of the letters below.

I and the Father are

one.

John 10:30

Ee

EVE

"Eve is the first woman God created"

EVE

eve

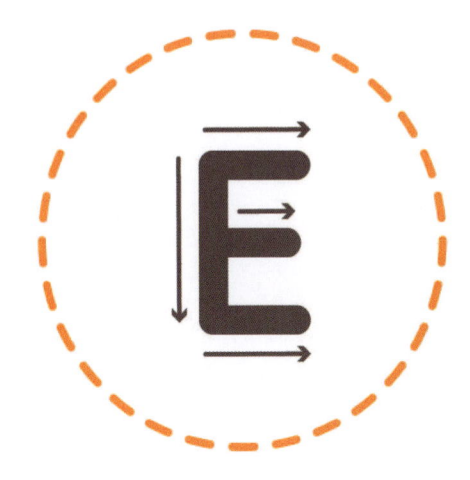

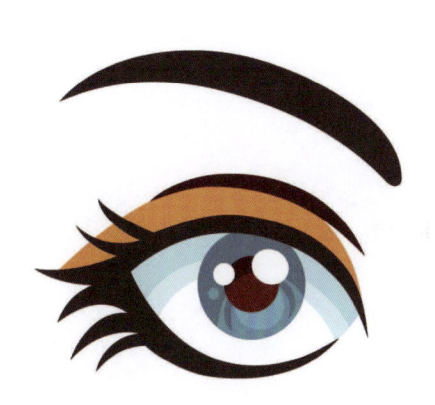

EYE

e

earth

Scripture of the day

Practice the scripture by tracing over each of the letters below.

This is the day which the Lord has made; Let's's rejoice and be glad in it. Psalm 118:24

Ff

FAITH

"Faith is trusting in God"

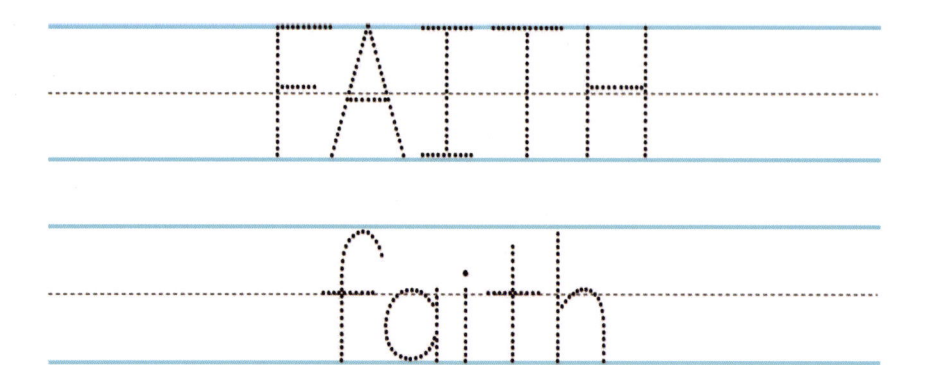

FAITH

faith

FIRE

fish

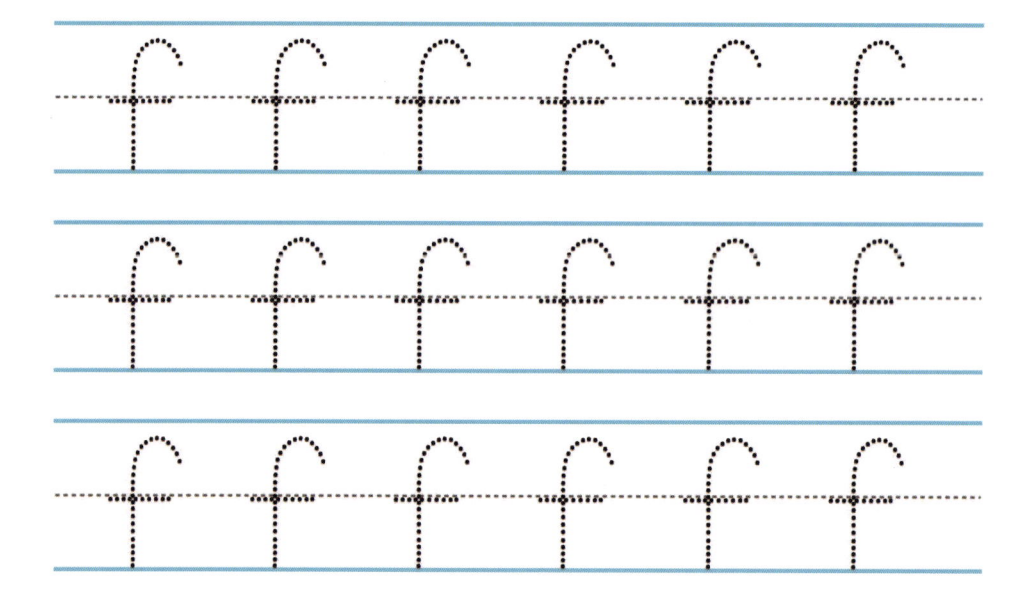

f f f f f f

f f f f f f

f f f f f f

Scripture of the day

Practice the scripture by tracing over each of the letters below.

Rejoice always.

Rejoice always.

Rejoice always.

1 Thessalonians 5:16

Gg

GOD

"God created the heavens and the earth"

GOD

god

G

GARDEN

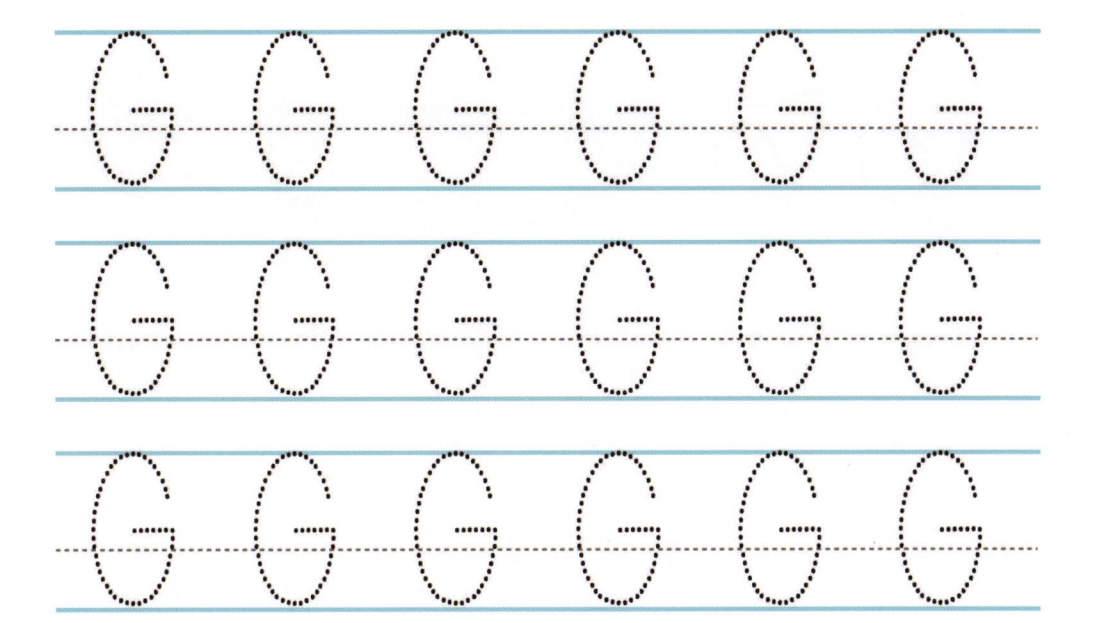

g

grapes

g g g g g g

g g g g g g

g g g g g g

Scripture of the day

Practice the scripture by tracing over each of the letters below.

Children, obey your parents in the Lord, for this is right.
Ephesians 6:1

Hh

HEAVEN

"God and His Angels stay in heaven"

HEAVEN

heaven

HOUSE

h

heart

Scripture of the day

Practice the scripture by tracing over each of the letters below.

The Lord is my light
and my salvation;
Whom should I fear?
Psalm 27:1

Ii

IDOL

"Christians don't worship idols"

IDOL

idol

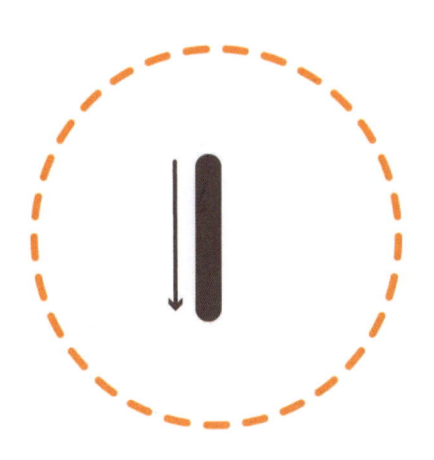

INN

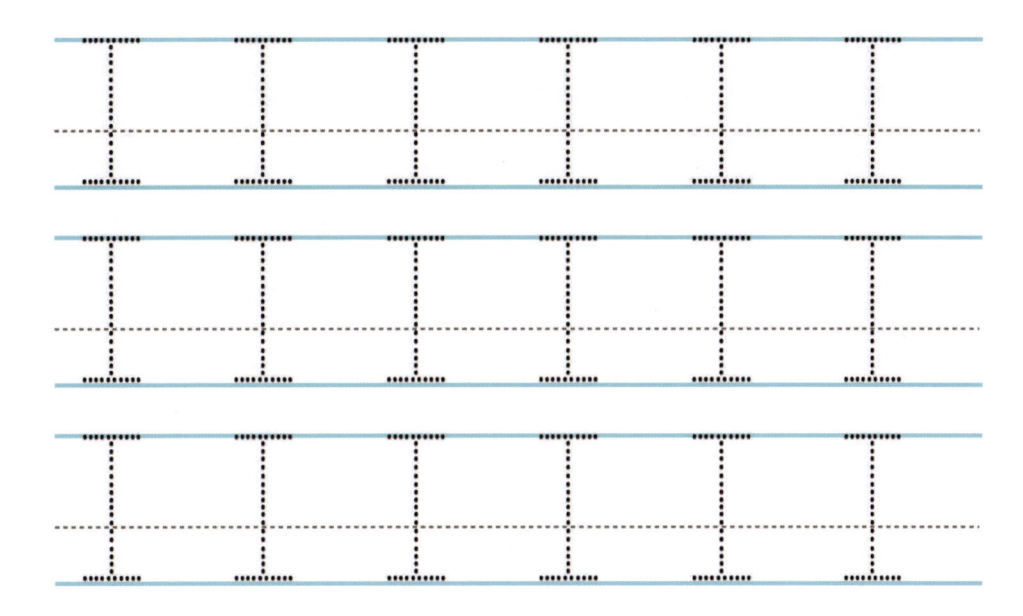

i

ice

Scripture of the day

Practice the scripture by tracing over each of the letters below.

Rejoice in the Lord always; again I say, rejoice !

Philippians 4:4

Jj

JESUS

"Jesus is the son of God.
He is known as Christ"

JESUS

jesus

JEWEL

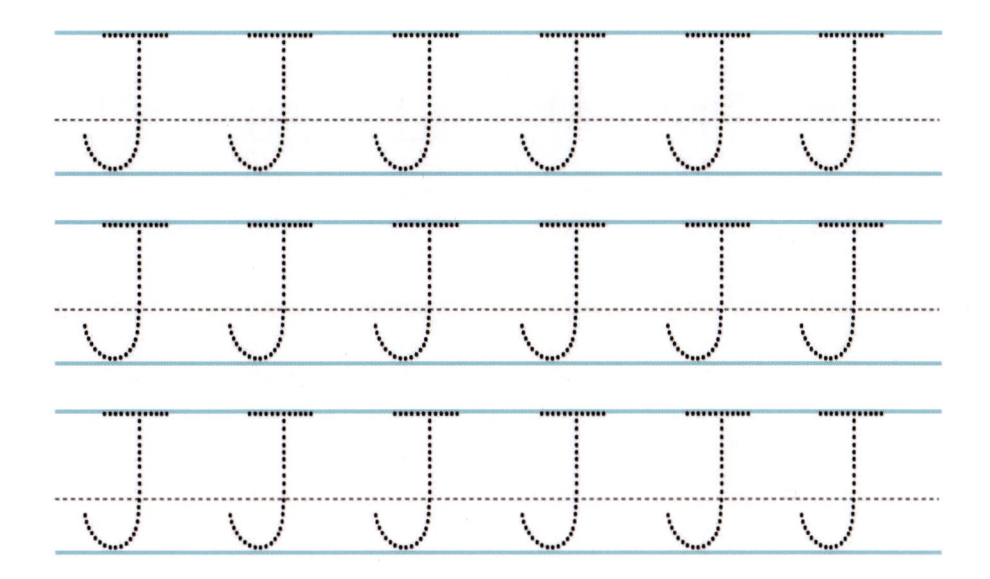

judge

j j j j j j
j j j j j j
j j j j j j

Scripture of the day

Practice the scripture by tracing over each of the letters below.

Pray without ceasing.

1 Thessalonians 5:17

Kk

KING

"A King is a man that rules a kingdom"

KING

king

K

KNOT

k

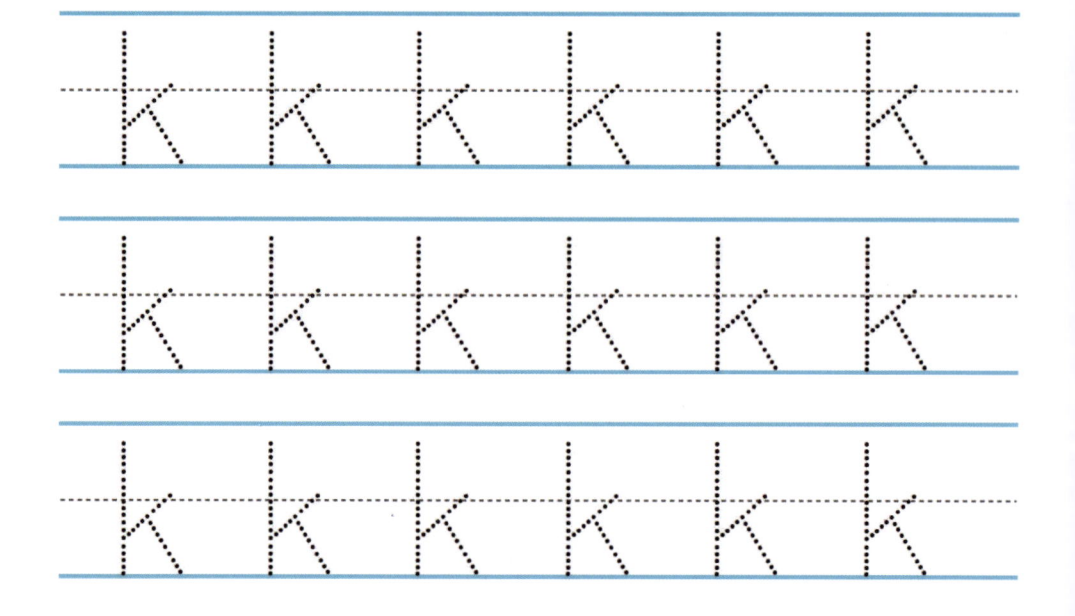

kettle

Scripture of the day

Practice the scripture by tracing over each of the letters below.

Jesus Christ is the
same yesterday and
today, and forever.
Hebrews 13:8

Ll

LORD

"Christians also call God Lord"

LORD

lord

LION

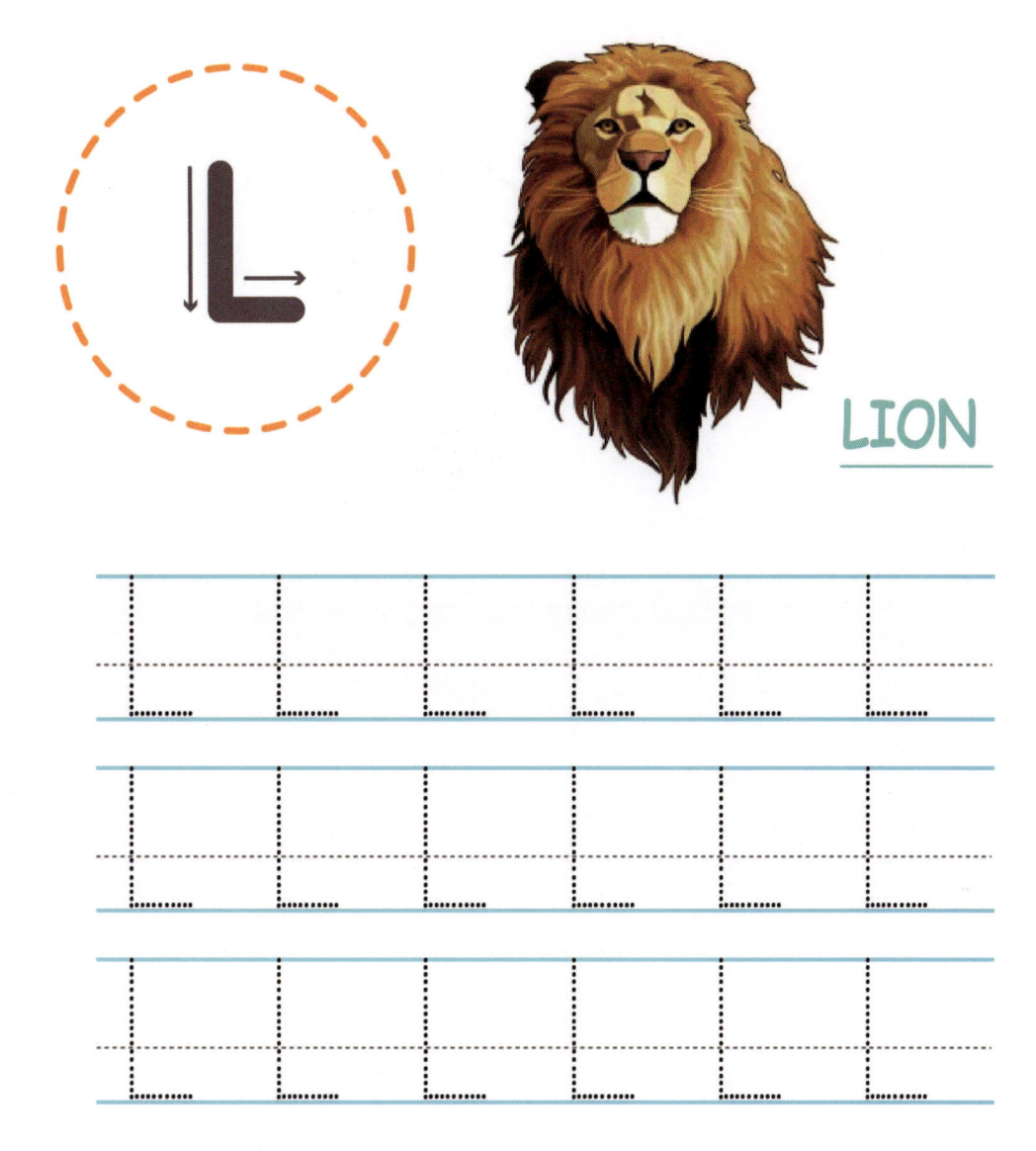

light

Scripture of the day

Practice the scripture by tracing over each of the letters below.

The Lord bless you,

and keep you.

Numbers 6:24

Mm   MARY

"Mary is the mother of Jesus Christ"

MARY

mary

MAN

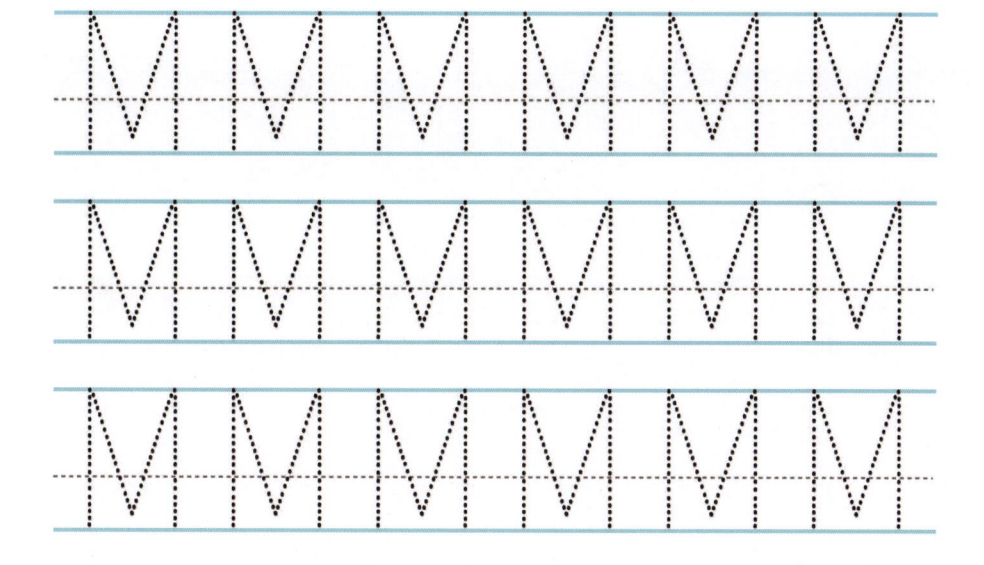

m

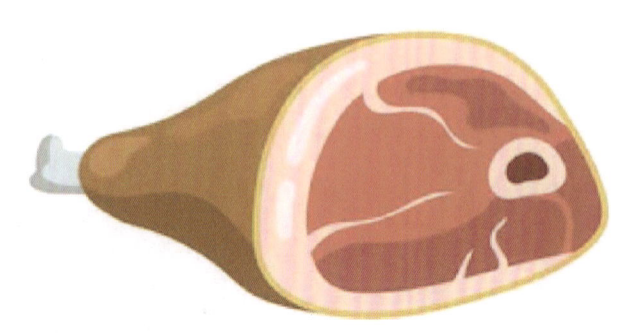

meat

mmmmmmmmm

mmmmmmmm

mmmmmmmm

Scripture of the day

Practice the scripture by tracing over each of the letters below.

In Him was life, and the life was the Light of mankind.

— John 1:4

Nn

NOAH

"Noah is the man
God told to build an ark"

NOAH

noah

NIGHT

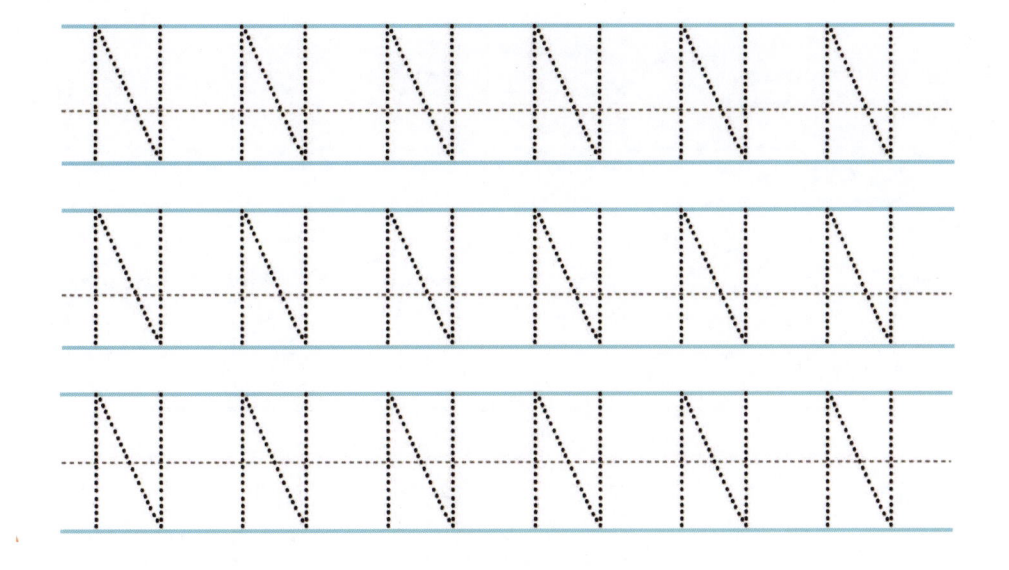

N N N N N
N N N N N
N N N N N

n

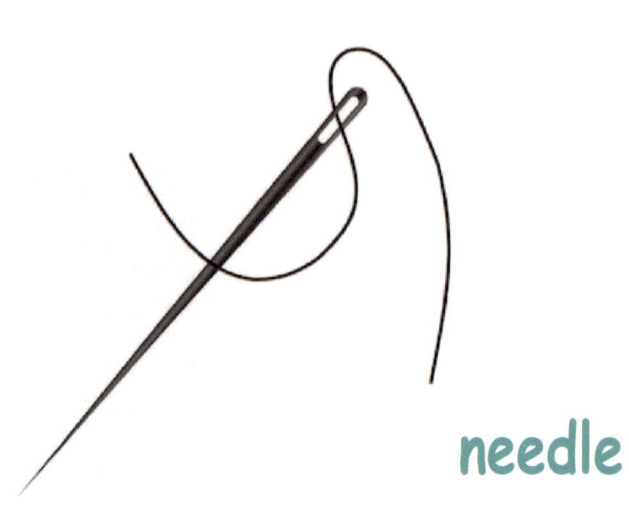

needle

n n n n n n

n n n n n n

n n n n n n

Scripture of the day

Practice the scripture by tracing over each of the letters below.

All that you do must be done in love.
1 Corinthians 16:14

Oo

OBEY

"Honor your father and mother"

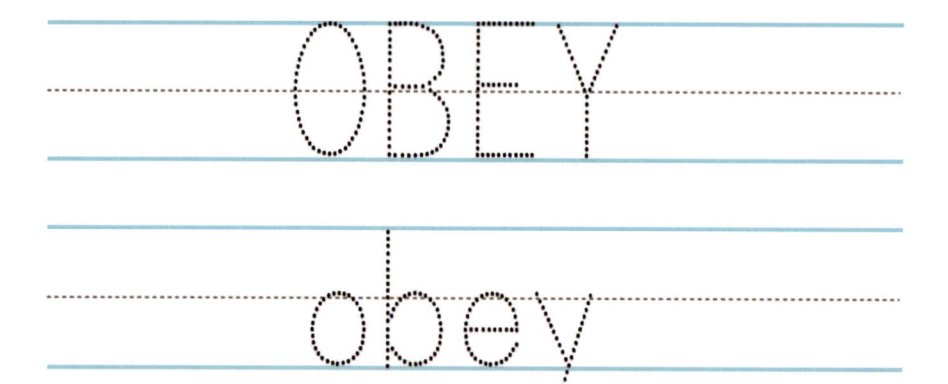

OBEY

obey

OLIVE

ox

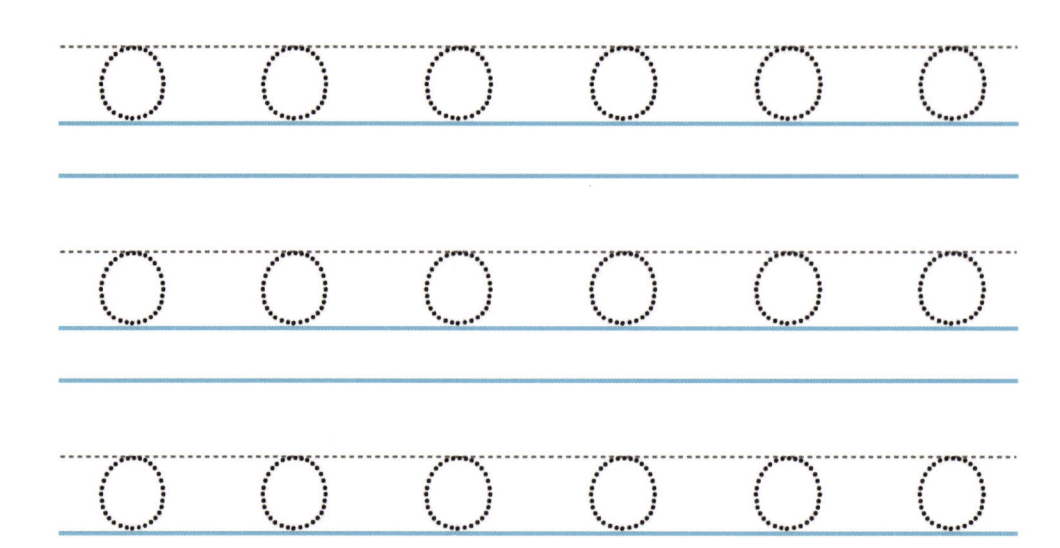

o o o o o o

o o o o o o

o o o o o o

Scripture of the day

Practice the scripture by tracing over each of the letters below.

When I am afraid,

I will put my trust

in You.

Psalm 56:3

Pp

PAUL

"Paul is an Apostle of Jesus Christ"

PAUL

paul

P

PILLAR

P P P P P P
P P P P P P
P P P P P P

p

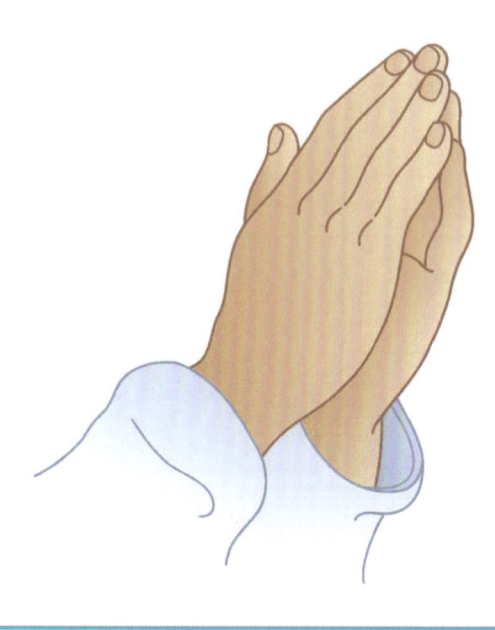

pray

p p p p p p

p p p p p p

p p p p p p

Scripture of the day

Practice the scripture by tracing over each of the letters below.

Behold, children are a gift of the Lord, The fruit of the womb is a reward.   Psalm 127:3

Qq

QUEEN

"A Queen is a woman that rules a kingdom"

QUEEN

queen

QUIET

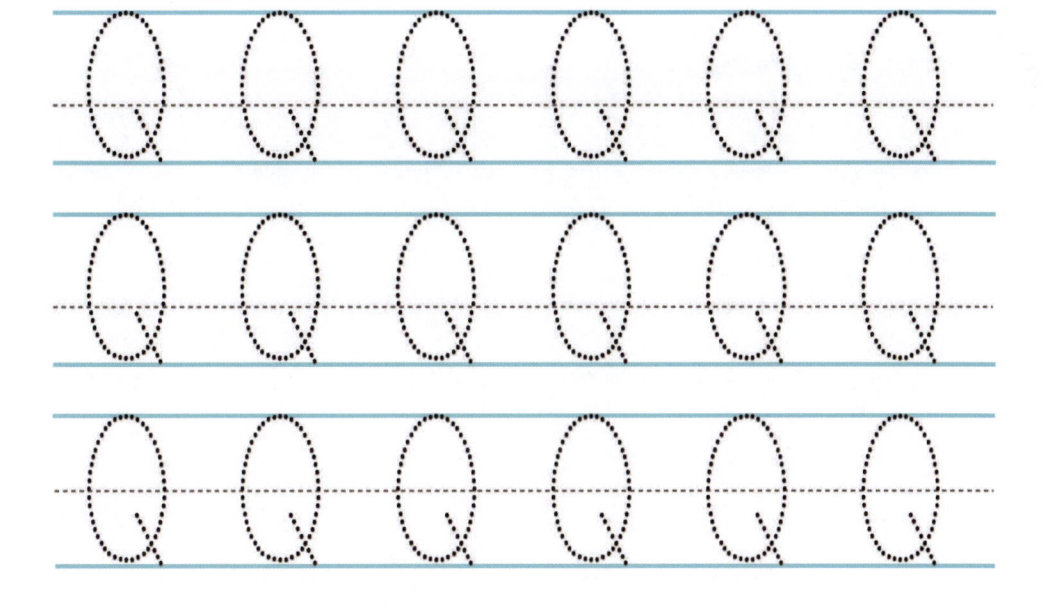

q

question

Scripture of the day

Practice the scripture by tracing over each of the letters below.

Brothers and sisters,

pray for us.

1 Thessalonians 5:25

Rr

RUTH

"Ruth was a loyal woman"

RUTH

ruth

R

RABBIT

R R R R R R
R R R R R R
R R R R R R

rainbow

r r r r r r

r r r r r r

r r r r r r

Scripture of the day

Practice the scripture by tracing over each of the letters below.

Your word is a lamp to my feet And a light to my path.

Psalm 119:105

Ss

SAINT

"A saint is a person that is holy to God"

SAINT

saint

S

STAR

S S S S S S
S S S S S S
S S S S S S

S

sun

S S S S S S

S S S S S S

S S S S S S

Scripture of the day

Practice the scripture by tracing over each of the letters below.

You shall have no other gods besides Me.

Deuteronomy 5:7

Tt

TRUTH

"Truth is a weapon that will always set you free"

TRUTH

truth

T

TIGER

tree

Scripture of the day

Practice the scripture by tracing over each of the letters below.

We love, because He first loved us.

1 John 4:19

Uu

UNITY

"Unity means being together as one"

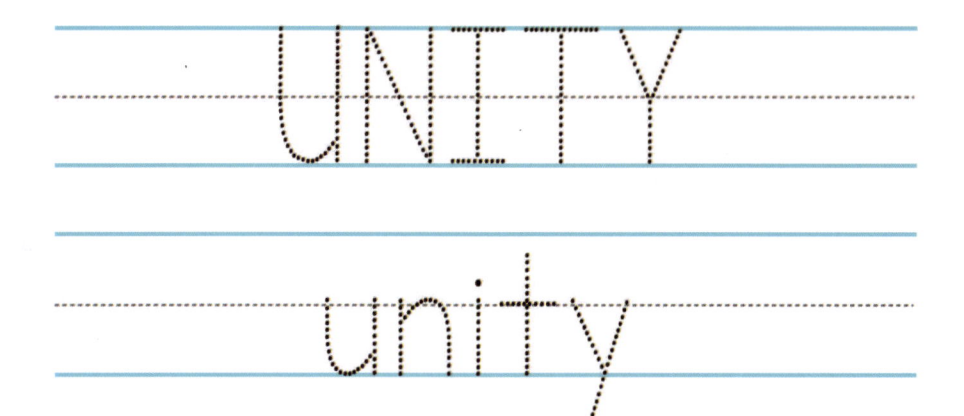

UNITY

unity

UNICORN

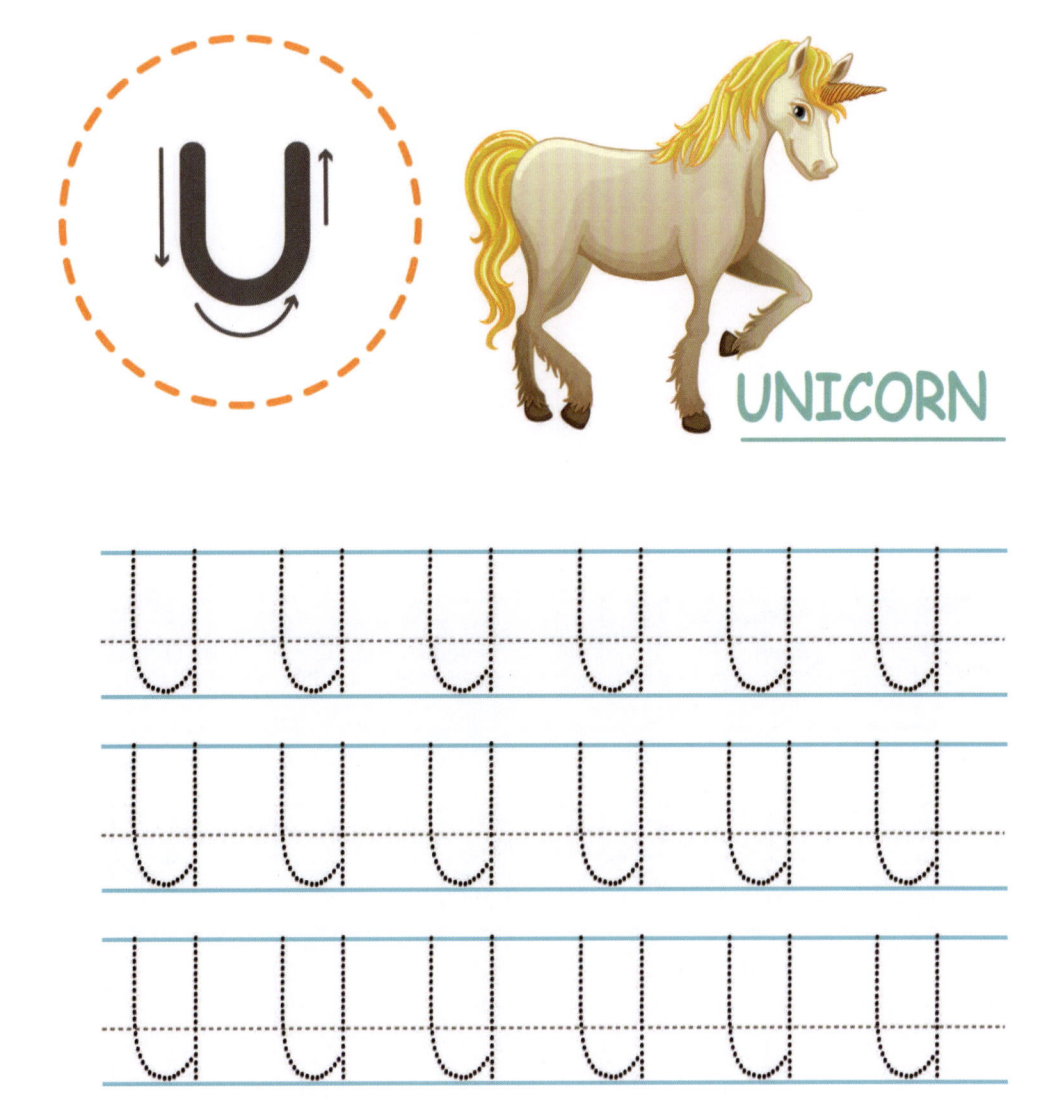

urn

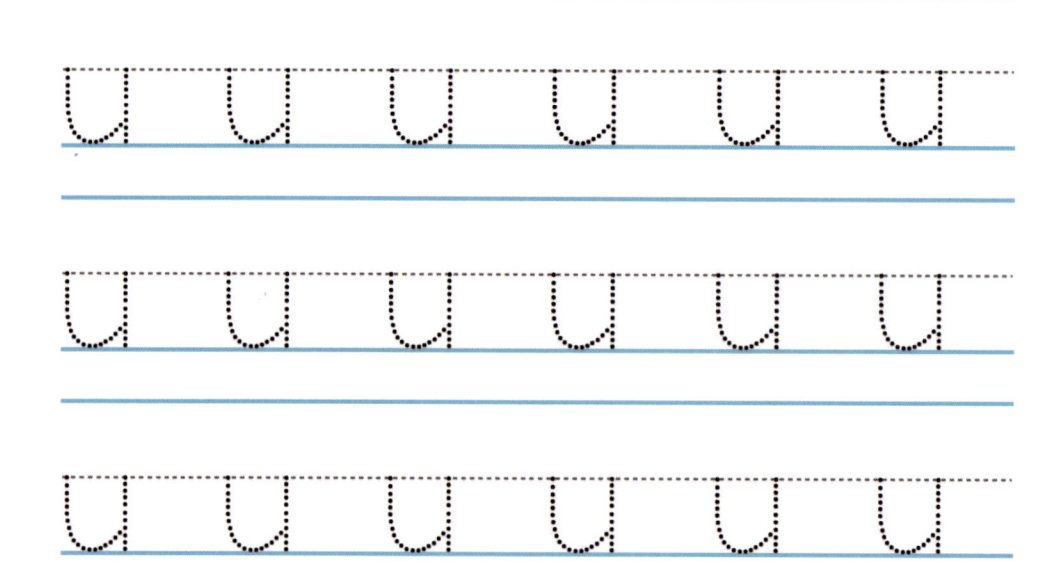

Scripture of the day

Practice the scripture by tracing over each of the letters below.

The second is like it,

"You shall love your

neighbor as yourself."

Matthew 22:39

Vv

VICTORY

"Victory is success over an obstacle"

VICTORY

victory

VIOLIN

vail

Scripture of the day

Practice the scripture by tracing over each of the letters below.

Everything that has
breath shall praise
the Lord.
Psalm 150:6

Ww

WORSHIP

"Worship means honoring and respecting God"

WORSHIP

worship

WORM

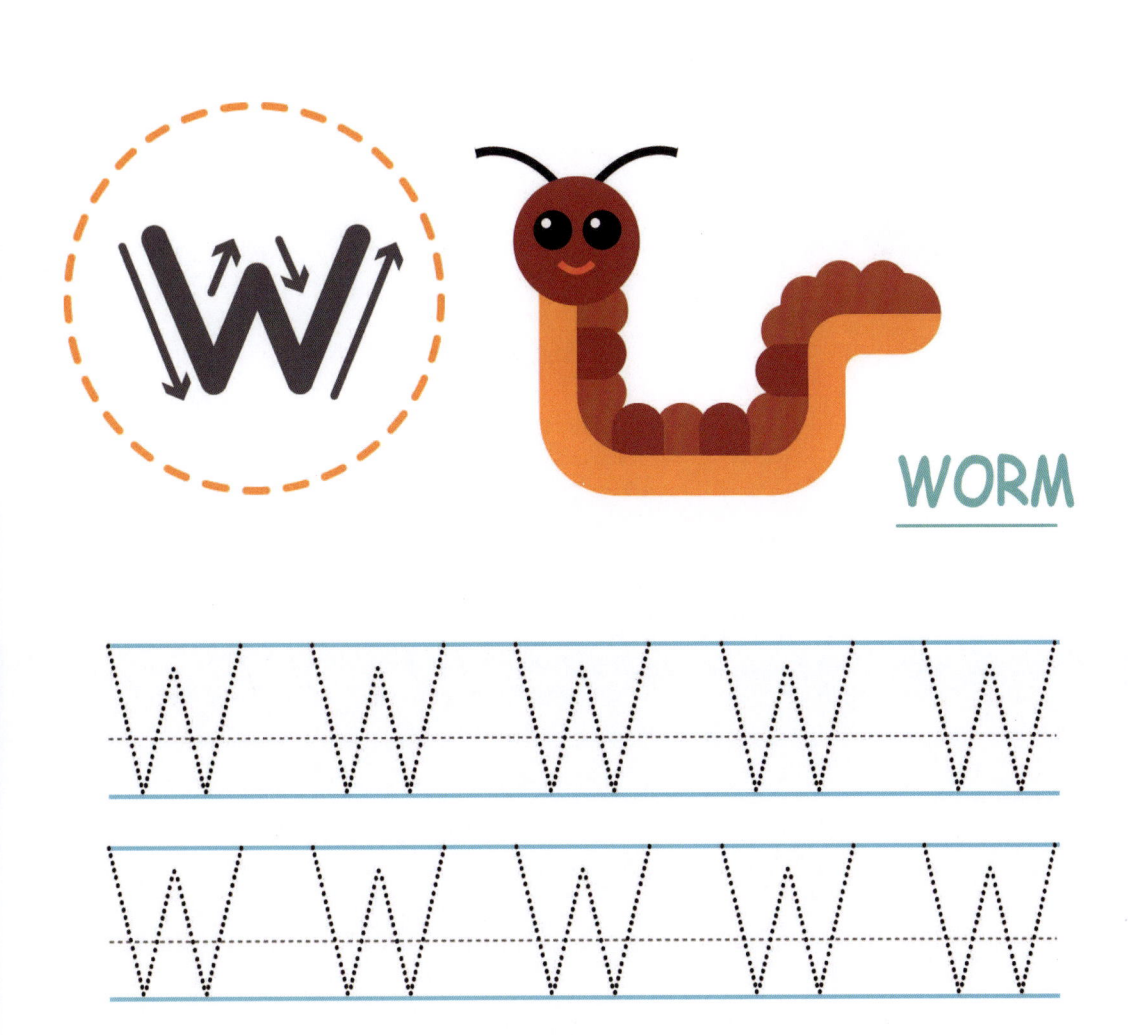

w

water

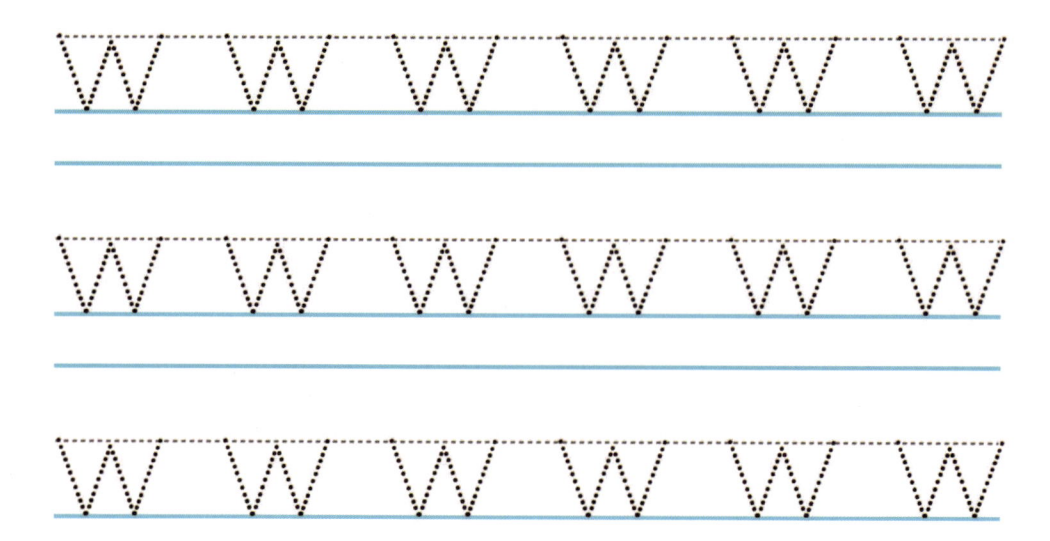

w w w w w w

w w w w w w

w w w w w w

Scripture of the day

Practice the scripture by tracing over each of the letters below.

for "Everyone who calls on the name of the Lord will be saved."

Romans 10:13

Xx

XERXES

"Xerxes was the king"

XERXES

xerxes

XERUS

xylophone

X X X X X X

X X X X X X

X X X X X X

Scripture of the day

Practice the scripture by tracing over each of the letters below.

Seek the Lord and His strength; Seek His face continually.
1 Chronicles 16:11

Yy

YAHWEH

"Yahweh is God in Hebrew language"

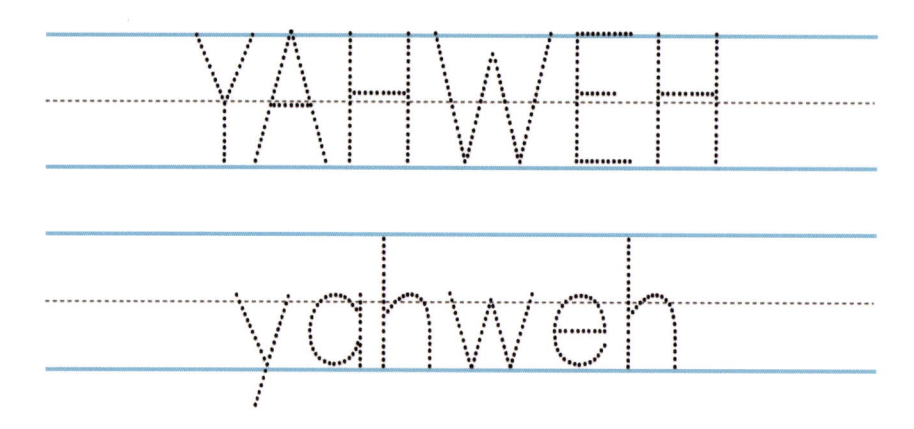

YAHWEH

yahweh

YARN

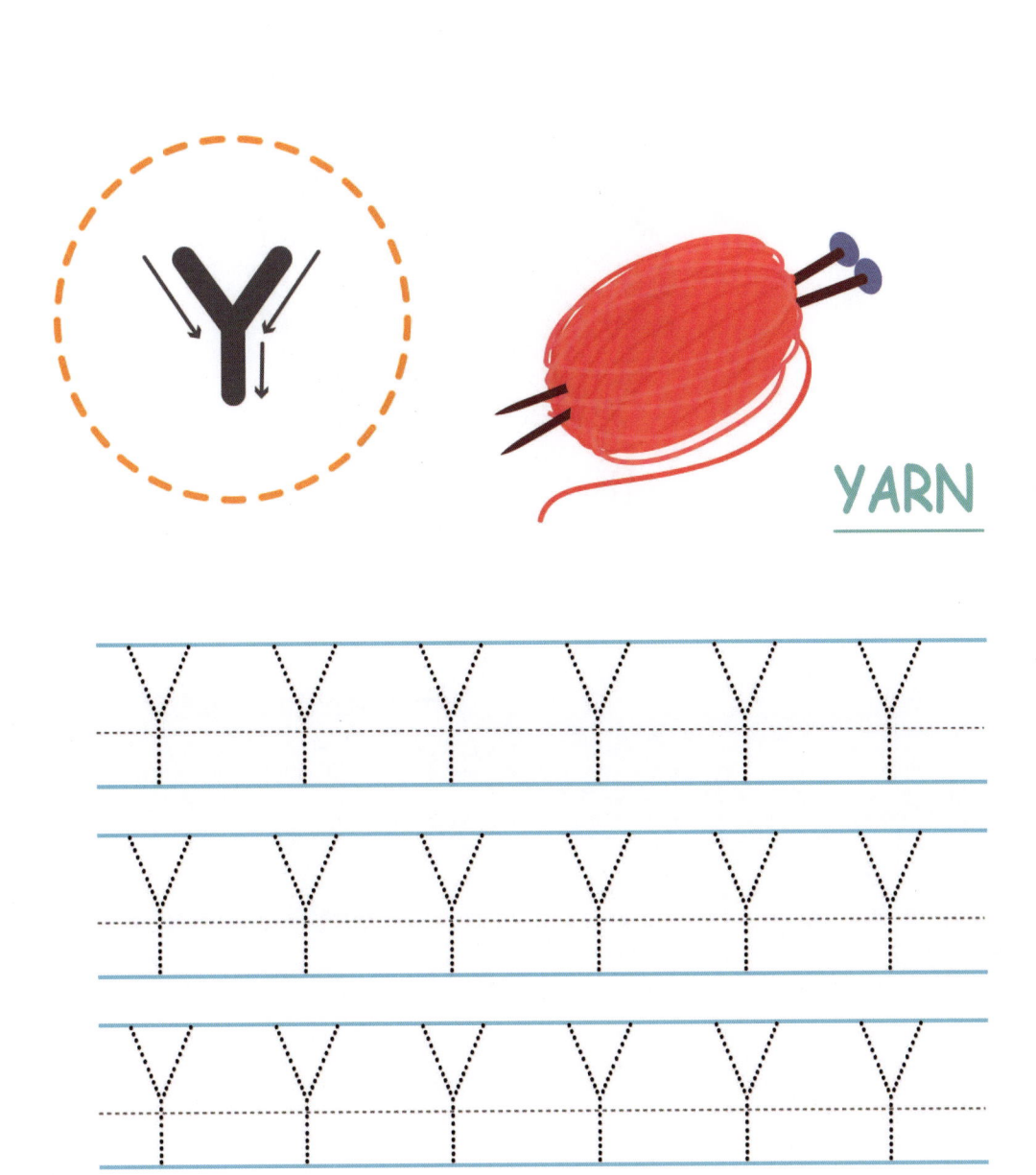

y

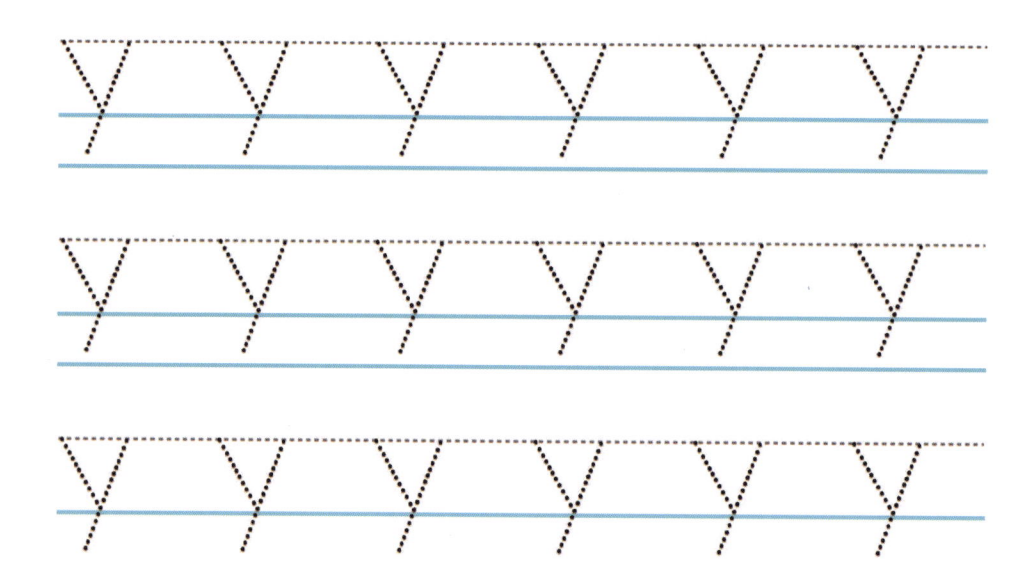

yak

y y y y y y

y y y y y y

y y y y y y

Scripture of the day

Practice the scripture by tracing over each of the letters below.

Set your minds on the things that are above, not on the things on earth.   Colossians 3:2

Zz

ZION

"Zion is a holy city"

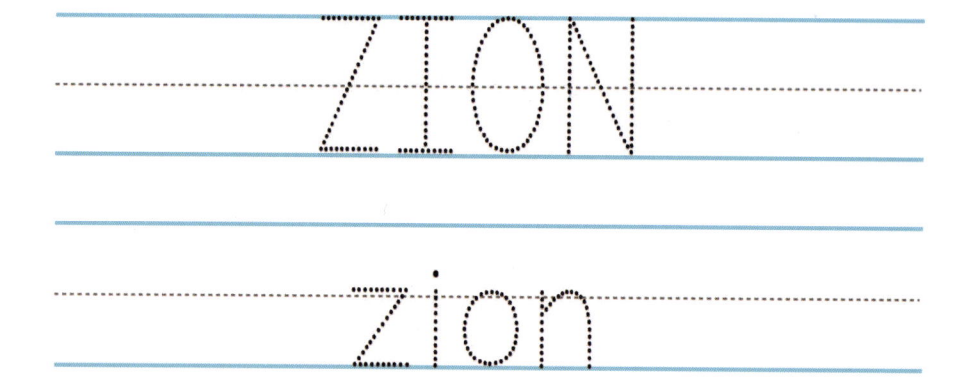

ZION

zion

ZIPPER

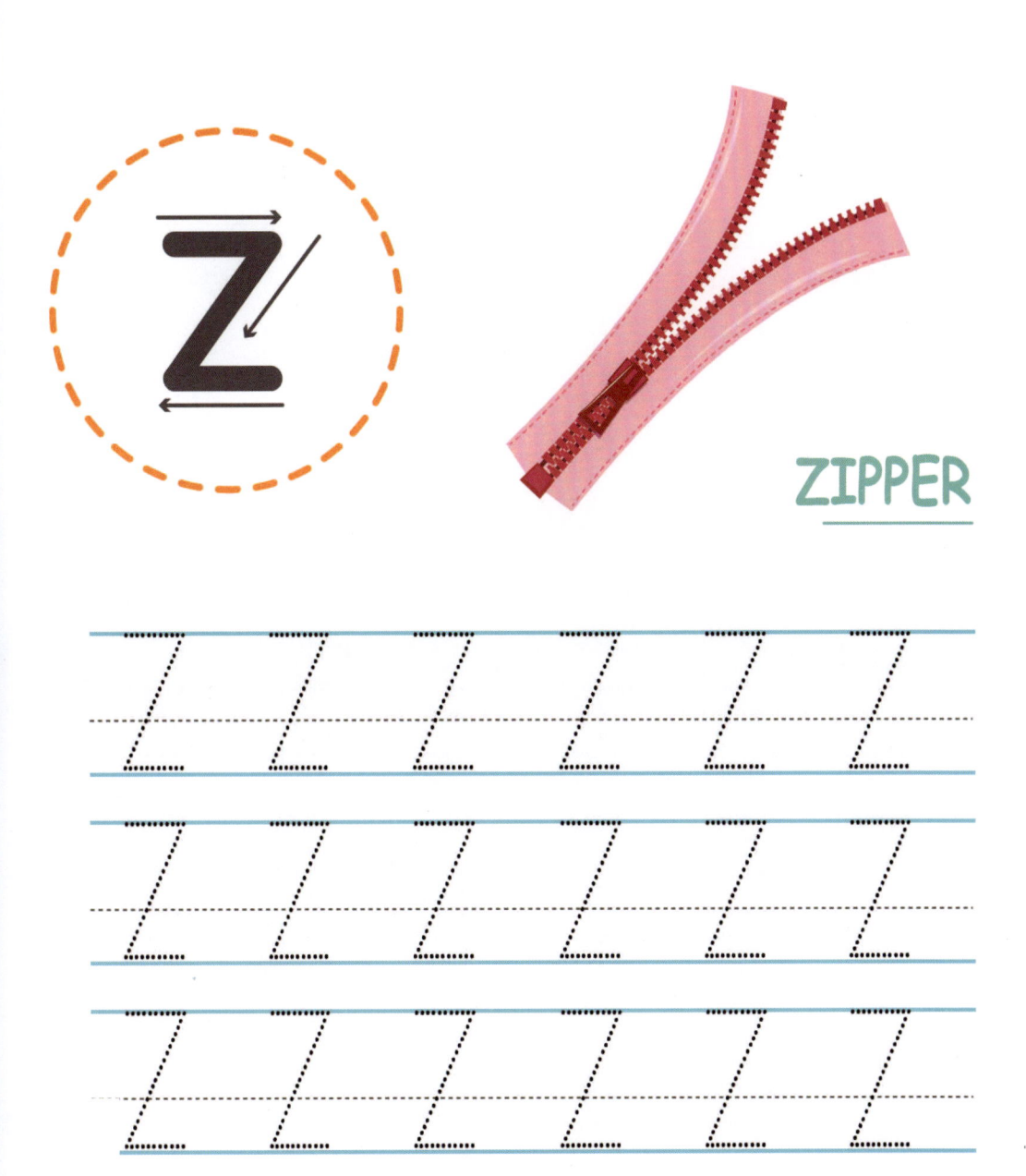

zebra

Scripture of the day

Practice the scripture by tracing over each of the letters below.

Children, obey your parents in everything, for this is pleasing to the Lord. Colossians 3:20

Dr. Tara Hines-McCoy is a Career Coach, professional development & diversity trainer, and public speaker. She has been featured in Dallas Weekly, on several podcasts, and graced the stage as a speaker at the American Mensa World Gathering.

Through her UP or OUT program, Dr. Tara is helping women take action and awaken their careers. She also enjoys motivating audiences of all sizes. As a former global human resources professional of fifteen years, she presents to leaders in an array of industries on influence and diversity topics.